I0788151

CHINESE IDIOM STORIES (PART 1)

成语故事

https://ChineseBull.com/

PREFACE

Idioms (成语, chéng yǔ) are a very important feature of the traditional Chinese culture. They are the stereotyped words in Chinese vocabulary. The idioms often have a fixed structure and statement to express deep meanings. Chinese idioms are applied as a whole in the sentences, and they bear the subject, object, attributes, and other components. Some idioms are just tiny sentences. In fact, most of the idioms are made of four characters, however, there are also three-character, five-character or even seven-character idioms in Mandarin Chinese language.

In Chinese language and culture, idioms are very popular. Most of the Chinese books, including primary level textbooks, contain numerous well-known contextual idioms. Without knowing Chinese idioms, it'd be difficult to read and understand the Chinese books. However, understanding the Chinese idioms itself can be a daunting task, especially for the foreigners and beginners. Most of the Chinese idioms have some sort of traditional stories associated with them. Once you understand those stories, related characters, and words, it'd be very convenient to understand the corresponding idioms.

As such, the idiom stories (成语故事, Chéngyǔ gùshì) are part of the Chinese history and culture (历史文化, Lìshǐ wénhuà). Behind every idiom is a story with far-reaching meaning, which is essentially the result of the crystallization of the wisdom of the ancient people of China for thousands of years. The characteristics of the idiom stories are profound and timeless. The idiom stories tell us certain facts with profound and vivid story allusions. By understanding Chinese idiom stories, you can understand Chinese history better. Hence, learning idioms is virtually essential for the foreigners to learn Chinese culture.

The books in *Chinese Idiom Story* series provide you numerous must-know and extremely popular Chinese idioms and their origin stories. Each story book, featuring about 8 to 10 famous stories, includes explanations of the idioms and their stories in both English and Chinese. The Chinese text of the story is slightly different from the English. In order to enforce deeper learning, the translation of the Chinese text is purposely not provided in the book. Further, the important words of the Chinese text have been listed before the main text. The book provides you simplified characters and pinyin for all the words and the main text. Also, the MP3 audios for the Chinese words and main text can be assessed from the home page of my website (https://ChineseBull.com/):

https://chinesebull.com/audio/idiom-stories/chinese-idiom-stories-1-audio-files/

<u>or</u>

https://bit.ly/38MoVkl

These links can be assessed without requiring any log in and password. In fact, these free audio lessons are the supplementary material to the main book.

If you don't understand some sounds or you think they are too fast for your Chinese listening abilities, you can leave feedback (say comments) on my site. I will consider posting new and updated audios.

Best wishes

Kexin Su

苏可馨

September 2021

Copyrights

CHINESE IDIOM STORIES

成语故事

Kexin Su

Acknowledgments

My sincere thanks to everyone, including my parents, friends, students, and teachers whose association and love enabled me to write this book.

I have often drawn inspiration from innocent kids -- and I sincerely convey my love to all of them.

I also thank my publishers to support me publish this book.

Contents

Idiom List

1	疑人偷斧	Yí rén tōu fǔ	Unfounded suspicion
2	爱鹤失众	Ài hè shī zhòng	Losing big because of love for the small
3	拔苗助长/ 揠苗助长	Bá miáo zhù zhǎng/ yà miáo zhù zhǎng	Haste makes waste
4	别无长物	Bié wú cháng wù	Living frugally
5	不可救药	Bù kě jiù yào	Incurable
6	捉襟见肘	Zhuō jīn jiàn zhǒu	Taking care of this and losing that
7	趾高气昂/ 趾高气扬	Zhǐ gāo qì'áng/ zhǐ gāo qì yáng	Arrogant
8	有备无患	Yǒu bèi wú huàn	Be prepared in advance
9	滥竽充数	Làn yú chōng shù	To fill a post without real qualifications

Chapter 1: Unfounded Suspicion.

Idiom: 疑人偷斧。

Pinyin: Yí rén tōu fǔ.

English: To suspects others without any basis; unfounded suspicion.

Source: From "Lu's Spring and Autumn".

出处:《吕氏春秋》。

Chūchù: "Lǚ shì chūnqiū".

疑	Yí	Doubt; disbelieve; suspect
人	Rén	Person; people
偷	Tōu	Steal; burglarize
斧	Fǔ	Axe; hatchet

English

Once upon a time, a farmer lost an axe. He suspected that it was a neighbor's kid who stole it, so he secretly started observing that kid. He looked at the child's walking posture as if he had stolen an axe; he observed the child's expression as if he had stolen the axe; he listened to the child's tone as if he had stolen the axe. In short, in the farmer's eyes, the child's every move was like he had stolen the axe.

Soon after, the farmer found the axe while digging the dirt pit. It turned out that he himself had forgotten the axe in the pit. Subsequently, he looked at the neighbor's child again, and the Child's every move did not look like he had stolen an axe.

中文

1	比喻	Bǐyù	Metaphor or simile; analogy; figure of speech; allegory
2	没有	Méiyǒu	Not have; there is not; be without; not so ...as
3	任何	Rènhé	Any; whichever; whatever
4	证据	Zhèngjù	Evidence; proof; testimony
5	怀疑	Huáiyí	Distrust; doubt; suspect; have a suspicion that
6	别人	Biérén	Other people; others; people

7	成语	Chéngyǔ	Set phrase; idiom; idioms and allusions
8	春秋	Chūnqiū	Spring and autumn; year; age; annals
9	从前	Cóngqián	Before; formerly; in the past; once upon a time
10	一个人	Yīgè rén	One
11	自己的	Zìjǐ de	Self
12	斧头	Fǔtóu	Axe; hatchet
13	小孩子	Xiǎoháizi	Small kid; little one
14	偷走	Tōu zǒu	Run off; rob; walk off with; mooch
15	偷偷	Tōutōu	Stealthily; secretly; covertly; on the sly
16	走路	Zǒulù	Walk; go on foot
17	不久之后	Bùjiǔ zhīhòu	Before long; soon after; shortly afterwards
18	找到了	Zhǎodàole	Eureka; Found; find
19	丢失	Diūshī	Lose
20	原来	Yuánlái	Original; former; in the first place
21	他自己	Tā zìjǐ	Himself
22	遗失	Yíshī	Lose
23	小孩	Xiǎo hái	Child
24	一言一行	Yī yán yīxíng	Every word and action; a word and an action; in all

			that one said and did
25	样子	Yàngzi	Appearance; shape
26	启发	Qǐfā	Arouse; inspire; illuminate; enlighten
27	毫无根据	Háo wú gēnjù	Be entirely groundless
28	仔细地	Zǐxì de	Carefully; closely; thoroughly
29	主观	Zhǔguān	Subjectivity; subjective
30	胡乱	Húluàn	Carelessly; casually; at random
31	猜疑	Cāiyí	Harbour suspicions; be suspicious; have misgivings
32	偏差	Piānchā	Deviation; offset; deflection; departure
33	认清	Rèn qīng	See clearly; recognize; get a clear understanding of
34	真相	Zhēnxiàng	Face; naked truth; truth; the actual state of affairs

译意：比喻没有任何证据就怀疑别人的人。

故事：这个成语是来自《吕氏春秋》里的一个故事，从前有一个人把自己的斧头弄丢了，他怀疑是住在他家附近的的小孩子偷走了，于是就偷偷观察这个孩子，感觉这个孩子无论是走路，说话，还是做其他的事情都像是偷了斧头的样子。然而，不久之后他在挖地的时候，找到了他之前丢失的那把斧头，原来是他自己遗失在土地里。于是，他再看这个小孩的时候，就觉得他的一言一行不再像是偷了斧头的样子了。

启发：人不能毫无根据地怀疑别人，要通过仔细地调查，主观上胡乱猜疑会导致错误和偏差，使人不能认清事实的真相。

Pinyin

Yì yì: Bǐyù méiyǒu rènhé zhèngjù jiù huáiyí biérén de rén.

Gùshì: Zhège chéngyǔ shì láizì "lǔ shì chūnqiū" lǐ de yīgè gùshì, cóngqián yǒuyī gèrén bǎ zìjǐ de fǔtóu nòng diūle, tā huáiyí shì zhù zài tā jiā fùjìn de de xiǎoháizi tōu zǒule, yúshì jiù tōutōu guānchá zhège háizi, gǎnjué zhège hái zǐ wúlùn shì zǒulù, shuōhuà, háishì zuò qítā de shìqíng dōu xiàng shì tōule fǔtóu de yàngzi. Rán'ér, bùjiǔ zhīhòu tā zài wā dì de shíhòu, zhǎodàole tā zhīqián diūshī dì nà bǎ fǔtóu, yuánlái shì tā zìjǐ yíshī zài tǔdì lǐ. Yúshì, tā zài kàn zhège xiǎo hái de shíhòu, jiù juédé tā de yī yán yīxíng bù zài xiàng shì tōule fǔtóu de yàngzile.

Qǐfā: Rén bùnéng háo wú gēnjùdì huáiyí biérén, yào tōngguò zǐxì dì diàochá, zhǔguān shàng húluàn cāiyí huì dǎozhì cuòwù hé piānchā, shǐ rén bùnéng rèn qīng shìshí de zhēnxiàng.

Chapter 2: Losing the Big

Idiom: 爱鹤失众。

Pinyin: Ài hè shī zhòng.

English: Love the crane to lose the crowd; because I fell in love with the crane, I lost the support of everyone; losing big because of love for the small.

From: "Zuo Zhuan. The Second Year of Min Gong.

出自《左传．闵公二年》。

Chūzì "zuǒ chuán. Mǐn gōng èr nián".

爱	Ài	Love; like; affection
鹤	Hè	Crane
失	Shī	Lose; miss; let slip
众	Zhòng	Crowd; many; numerous; a lot of

English

During the Spring and Autumn Period, Wei Yi (卫懿公) of Wei Guo (卫国, Wei Kingdome) raised a lot of cranes. The officials of the court had to admire and show love for these cranes on a daily basis. The more cranes they admired, the happier the king was. The northern country of Yan heard the news that Wei Yi loved cranes, and sent him dozens of very rare cranes. When Wei Yi heard this, he was very happy. He traveled around the country and told the people that these cranes showed how powerful and rich Wei Guo was. Just when Wei Yi was boasting that he was rich, the Di people (狄人, Di, a term given to the northern tribes in ancient China) from neighboring countries sent troops to invade the Wei Guo, and Wei Yi ordered the countrymen to go to the frontline to respond to the enemy. However, at this time, people complained at the back: Didn't you mean that cranes are the most powerful and capable? Then let the cranes go to the frontline to repel the Di army, we love our country but we have no strength to fight. Finally, Wei Yi led the troops to meet the enemy, but the soldiers had no intention of fighting. Wei Yi finally died in the battle, and the country was perished.

中文

1	比喻	Bǐyù	Metaphor or simile; analogy; figure of speech; allegory
2	没有	Méiyǒu	Because; for; on account of
3	任何	Rènhé	Thing; object; arrangement
4	证据	Zhèngjù	Lose
5	利益	Lìyì	Interest; gain; benefit; profit
6	故事	Gùshì	Story; tale; plot; old practice; routine
7	在古代	Zài gǔdài	In ancient times; in the old days; in the ancient time
8	君王	Jūnwáng	King; lord
9	非常喜欢	Fēicháng xǐhuān	Like … Very much; Very much; I like it very much
10	思考	Sīkǎo	Think deeply; ponder over; reflect on; deliberate
11	更加	Gèngjiā	To a higher degree; still

			further; still more
12	富强	Fùqiáng	Prosperous and strong; thriving and powerful; rich and mighty
13	而是	Ér shì	Not A, but B
14	很多	Hěnduō	A lot of; a great many of; a good many of
15	心思	Xīnsī	Thought; idea
16	百姓	Bǎixìng	Common people; people
17	怨声载道	Yuànshēngzàidào	Voices of discontent are heard everywhere;
18	荒唐	Huāngtáng	Absurd; fantastic; preposterous; grossly exaggerated
19	官职	Guānzhí	Government post; official position
20	官员	Guānyuán	Official
21	享受	Xiǎngshòu	Enjoyment; comfort; fruition; treat
22	俸禄	Fènglù	An official's salary
23	敌国	Díguó	Enemy state; hostile country; hostile power
24	乘机	Chéngjī	Seize the opportunity
25	攻打	Gōngdǎ	Attack; assault; assail
26	过来	Guòlái	Come over; come up; can manage

27	灭亡	Mièwáng	Be destroyed; become extinct; perish; die out
28	做人	Zuòrén	Conduct oneself; behave
29	贪图	Tāntú	Seek; hanker after; covet
30	玩乐	Wánlè	Have fun; entertain (or amuse) oneself; make fun
31	耽误	Dānwù	Delay; hold up
32	事情	Shìqíng	Affair; matter; thing; business
33	切勿	Qiè wù	Be sure not to
34	因小失大	Yīn xiǎo shī dà	Lose a great deal through trying to save a little

译意：比喻因为小的事物而失去大的利益。

故事：在古代，有一位君王，非常喜欢养鹤。他每天不去思考如何将自己的国家建设得更加富强，而是花很多心思在养鹤上，百姓怨声载道。他甚至荒唐到给鹤封官职，像正常的官员一样享受俸禄。敌国乘机攻打过来，将他的国家灭亡。

启发：做人不能因为贪图玩乐而耽误自己重要的事情，切勿因小失大。

Pinyin

Yì yì: Bǐyù yīnwèi xiǎo de shìwù ér shīqù dà de lìyì.

Gùshì: Zài gǔdài, yǒuyī wèi jūnwáng, fēicháng xǐhuān yǎng hè. Tā měitiān bù qù sīkǎo rúhé jiāng zìjǐ de guójiā jiànshè dé gèngjiā fùqiáng, ér shì huā hěnduō xīnsī zài yǎng hè shàng, bǎixìng yuànshēngzàidào. Tā shènzhì huāngtáng dào gěi hè fēng guānzhí, xiàng zhèngcháng de guānyuán yīyàng xiǎngshòu fènglù. Díguó chéngjī gōngdǎ guòlái, jiāng tā de guójiā mièwáng.

Qǐfā: Zuòrén bùnéng yīnwèi tāntú wánlè ér dānwù zìjǐ zhòngyào de shìqíng, qiè wù yīn xiǎo shī dà.

Chapter 3: Haste Makes Waste

Idiom: 拔苗助长/揠苗助长。
Pinyin: Bá miáo zhù zhǎng/yà miáo zhù zhǎng.
English: Try to help the shoots grow by pulling them upward; spoil things by excessive enthusiasm; haste makes waste.
Source: "Mencius·Gongsun Chou".
出处:《孟子·公孙丑上》。
Chūchù: "Mèngzǐ·gōngsūn chǒu shàng".

拔	Bá	Pluck; pull out; pull up
揠	Yà	Pull up; tug upward
苗	Miáo	Seedling; sprout
助	Zhù	Help; support
长	Zhǎng	Grow; begin to grow; older; elder

English

In ancient times, there was a farmer in the Song State (宋国) who planted seedlings (禾苗)

in the field. After planting it, he went to the field all day long to observe the growth of the planted seedlings. After observing day after day, the farmer felt very anxious when he saw that there was no change in the seedlings. He thought about it and found a way to help the seedlings grow taller fast.

The farmer pulled up his trouser legs and went down to the field, pulling up the seedlings one by one. After tirelessly working for the whole day, the farmer returned home contentedly thinking about the instantly grown seedlings.

When he got home, he happily told his family: "It made me tired, but the seedlings finally grew a lot taller." The farmer's son ran to the field and found that the seedlings in the field were all dead.

中文

1	禾苗	Hémiáo	Seedlings of cereal crops; grain seedling; rice shoots

2	生长	Shēngzhǎng	Grow; grow up; ascent
3	比喻	Bǐyù	Metaphor or simile; analogy; figure of speech; allegory
4	顺应	Shùnyìng	Comply with; conform to; adjustment
5	客观事物	Kèguān shìwù	Objective things/reality
6	法则	Fǎzé	Rule; law
7	事情	Shìqíng	Affair; matter; thing; business
8	十分	Shífēn	Very; fully; utterly; extremely
9	急躁	Jízào	Irritable; irascible; testy
10	想要	Xiǎng yào	Want; intend; wish
11	更加	Gèngjiā	To a higher degree; still further; still more
12	糟糕	Zāogāo	How terrible; what bad luck; too bad
13	来源于	Láiyuán yú	Originate; stem from; root in
14	孟子	Mèngzǐ	Mencius
15	从前	Cóngqián	Before; formerly; in the past; once upon a time
16	农民	Nóngmín	Peasant; peasantry; farmer; boor; husbandman
17	田地	Tiándì	Field; farmland
18	担心	Dānxīn	Worry; feel anxious
19	于是	Yúshì	Thereupon; hence; consequently; as a result

20	天天	Tiāntiān	Every day; daily; day in, day out
21	好像	Hǎoxiàng	Seem; be like
22	一点也	Yīdiǎn yě	No way; on earth
23	长高	Zhǎng gāo	Raise oneself; grow taller; Get taller
24	想办法	Xiǎng bànfǎ	Think of a way; try to find a solution
25	帮助	Bāngzhù	Help; aid; assist; assistance
26	来到	Lái dào	Arrive; come
27	田地	Tiándì	Field; farmland
28	从早到晚	Cóng zǎo dào wǎn	From morning to night; from dawn till sundown; from sunup to sundown
29	终于	Zhōngyú	At last; in the end; finally; eventually
30	所有	Suǒyǒu	Own; possess; possessions; all
31	起来	Qǐlái	Stand up; sit up; rise to one's feet
32	拔高	Bágāo	Raise
33	回家	Huí jiā	Go home; be home; return home
34	回到家	Huí dàojiā	Get home; go back home; get in
35	家人	Jiārén	Family member; servant
36	长高	Zhǎng gāo	Raise oneself; grow taller; Get

			taller
37	儿子	Érzi	Son
38	急急忙忙	Jí ji máng mang	Hurried and busy; in a rush; in great haste; on the rush
39	跑到	Pǎo dào	Run to
40	枯死	Kūsǐ	Wither; dry up and die
41	对待	Duìdài	Treat; approach; handle; be in a position related to or compared with another
42	任何	Rènhé	Any; whichever; whatever
43	尊重	Zūnzhòng	Respect; value; esteem; make much of
44	客观	Kèguān	Objective
45	变化	Biànhuà	Change; variety; transformation; variation
46	规律	Guīlǜ	Law; regular pattern
47	违反	Wéifǎn	Violate; run counter to; transgress; infringe
48	将会	Jiāng huì	Will; would; shall; will be
49	得到	Dédào	Get; obtain; gain; receive

译意：将禾苗拔起，助其生长。比喻不顺应客观事物发展变化的法则，做事情十分急躁，想要快速完成，但是却把事情弄得更加糟糕。

故事：来源于《孟子》，从前宋国有一个农民，他在田地里种了禾苗，但是他担心自己的禾苗长不高，于是天天去看。他每天到田地里发现自己的禾苗好像一点也没有长高，于是想办法帮助禾苗生长。他来到田地里，一颗一颗将禾苗拔起一大截，从早到晚，终于把所有的禾苗都拔起来一大截，他看着拔高的禾苗高高兴兴地回家去了。回到家他告诉家人自己今天想办法让禾苗都长高了一大截，他的儿子急急忙忙跑到田地里看，发现所有的禾苗都枯死了。

启发：对待任何事情都要尊重其客观发展变化的规律，违反规律将会得到不好的结果。

Pinyin

Yì yì: Jiāng hémiáo bá qǐ, zhù qí shēngzhǎng. Bǐyù bù shùnyìng kèguān shìwù fāzhǎn biànhuà de fǎzé, zuò shìqíng shífēn jízào, xiǎng yào kuàisù wánchéng, dànshì què bǎ shìqíng nòng dé gèngjiā zāogāo.

Gùshì: Láiyuán yú "mèngzǐ", cóngqián sòng guóyǒu yīgè nóngmín, tā zài tiándì lǐ zhǒngle hémiáo, dànshì tā dānxīn zìjǐ de hémiáo cháng bù gāo, yúshì tiāntiān qù kàn. Tā měitiān dào tiándì lǐ fāxiàn zìjǐ de hémiáo hǎoxiàng yīdiǎn yě méiyǒu zhǎng gāo, yúshì xiǎng bànfǎ bāngzhù hémiáo shēngzhǎng. Tā lái dào tiándì lǐ, yī kē yī kē jiāng hémiáo bá qǐ yī dà jié, cóng zǎo dào wǎn, zhōngyú bǎ suǒyǒu de hémiáo dōu bá qǐlái yī dà jié, tā kànzhe bágāo de hémiáo gāo gāoxìng xìng de huí jiā qùle. Huí dàojiā tā gàosù jiārén zìjǐ jīntiān xiǎng bànfǎ ràng hémiáo dōu zhǎng gāole yī dà jié, tā de érzi jí ji máng mang pǎo dào tiándì lǐ kàn, fāxiàn suǒyǒu de hémiáo dōu kūsǐle.

Qǐfā: Duìdài rènhé shìqíng dōu yào zūnzhòng qí kèguān fāzhǎn biànhuà de guīlǜ, wéifǎn guīlǜ jiāng huì dédào bù hǎo de jiéguǒ.

Chapter 4: Living Frugally

Idiom: 别无长物。

Pinyin: Bié wú cháng wù.

English: Empty; there was nothing precious; be poorly off; have no other possessions than one's own self; have nothing except the bare necessities at home; living frugally; poverty.

Source: "Book of Jin • Biography of Wang Gong.

出处：《晋书•王恭传》。

Chūchù: "Jìn shū•wánggōngchuán".

别	Bié	Other; another; some other
无	Wú	Not have; there is not; nil
长	Cháng	Lasting; long; be good at
物	Wù	Thing; object

English

In the Eastern Jin Dynasty (东晋), there was a scholar named Wang Gong (王恭) who lived a frugal and simple life.

One year, Wang Gong followed his father from Kuaiji (会稽/会稽郡, in the modern Wu County of Suzhou City, Jiangsu Province) to the capital city of Jiankang (建康, ancient name for Nanjing), and his friend, Wang Chen (王忱), came to visit him. Wang Chen felt that the bamboo mats on the ground were very good.

Because Kuaiji was rich in bamboo mats (竹席), he thought Wang Gong must have brought a lot of them, so he asked Wang Gong to give him one.

Wang Gong gave this bamboo mat on the ground to Wang Chen. After giving it away, he started using grassmat (草席). Later, Wang Chen found out and came to Wang Gong to apologize. Wang Gong smiled and said: "You don't know me very well. I don't have any extras (多余, more than what is required; superfluous things) in my life".

中文

1	一个人	Yīgè rén	One
2	除了	Chúle	Except
3	之外	Zhī wài	Besides; except; beyond
4	没有	Méiyǒu	Not have; there is not; be without; not so ...as
5	其他	Qítā	Other; else
6	现在	Xiànzài	Now; at present; today; nowadays
7	形容	Xíngróng	Appearance; countenance
8	贫困	Pínkùn	Poor; impoverished; poverty-stricken; in straitened circumstances
9	来源于	Láiyuán yú	Originate; stem from; root in
10	时候	Shíhòu	Time
11	读书人	Dúshūrén	Scholar; intellectual
12	他的名字	Tā de míngzì	His name
13	从来	Cónglái	Always; at all times; all along
14	贪图	Tāntú	Seek; hanker after; covet
15	享受	Xiǎngshòu	Enjoyment; comfort; fruition; treat

16	极其	Jíqí	Most; extremely; exceedingly
17	朴素	Púsù	Simple; plain
18	生活	Shēnghuó	Life; live; exist; livelihood
19	读书人	Dúshūrén	Scholar; intellectual
20	人们	Rénmen	People; men; the public; humanity
21	觉得	Juédé	Feel; be aware; sense
22	将来	Jiānglái	Future
23	一定	Yīdìng	Fixed; established; regular
24	厉害	Lìhài	Severe; sharp; cruel; fierce
25	人物	Rénwù	Figure; personage; person in literature; character
26	有一次	Yǒu yīcì	Once; on one occasion
27	他的	Tā de	His; him; he; his
28	父亲	Fùqīn	Father
29	外地	Wàidì	Other places; nonlocal; parts of the country other than where one is
30	老乡	Lǎoxiāng	Fellow-townsman; fellow-villager
31	过来	Guòlái	Come over; come up; can manage
32	看望	Kànwàng	Call on; visit; see; look-in´
33	十分	Shífēn	Very; fully; utterly; extremely

34	开心	Kāixīn	Feel happy; rejoice; joyful; be delighted
35	觉得	Juédé	Feel; be aware; sense
36	竹席	Zhú xí	Bamboo mat
37	舒服	Shūfú	Comfortable
38	心里	Xīnlǐ	In the heart; at heart; in mind
39	盛产	Shèngchǎn	Abound in; teem with
40	家乡	Jiāxiāng	Hometown; homeplace; native place
41	于是	Yúshì	Thereupon; hence; consequently; as a result
42	感觉	Gǎnjué	Sense perception; sensation; feeling;
43	立马	Lìmǎ	Pull up a horse
44	明白	Míngbái	Clear; obvious; plain
45	意思	Yìsi	Meaning; idea
46	送给	Sòng gěi	Send/present to
47	很高兴	Hěn gāoxìng	Delighted; very happy; With pleasure
48	回家	Huí jiā	Go home; be home; return home
49	其实	Qíshí	Actually; in fact; as a matter of fact; really
50	只有	Zhǐyǒu	Only; alone
51	带走	Dài zǒu	Take/bring away

52	草席	Cǎo xí	Grassmat; petate; straw mat
53	睡觉	Shuìjiào	Sleep; fall asleep; go to bed; have a sleep
54	得知	Dé zhī	Be informed of
55	事情	Shìqíng	Affair; matter; thing; business
56	心里	Xīnlǐ	In the heart; at heart; in mind
57	过意不去	Guòyìbùqù	Feel apologetic; feel sorry
58	去找	Qù zhǎo	Go for; look for; to call for
59	道歉	Dàoqiàn	Apologize; make an apology
60	一生	Yīshēng	A lifetime; all one's life; throughout one's life

译意：比喻一个人除了自己的身上之外没有其他多余的东西。现在用来形容人的贫困。

故事：来源于《晋书》。在古时候，有一个读书人，他的名字叫王恭，他从来都不贪图享受，过着极其朴素的生活。人们觉得他将来一定能成为一个厉害的人物。有一次，他的父亲带着他去了外地，有一个老乡过来看望他，他们聊得十分开心。聊着聊着这位老乡觉得坐着的竹席很舒服，他心里想王恭从盛产竹席的家乡过来，一定带了很多这样的竹席，于是想问他要一张竹席。就说："这个竹席坐着感觉很舒服。"，王恭立马明白了他的意思，笑着说："那就把这个送给你吧。"老乡很高兴地把竹席带回家了。其实王恭只有这一个竹席，老乡把竹席带走后，他就用草席睡觉。老乡得知了这件事情之后，心里感觉很过意不去，就去找王恭道歉，王恭笑着说："你可能不太了解我，我这一生没有太多的多余的东西。"

Pinyin

Yì yì: Bǐyù yīgè rén chúle zìjǐ de shēnshang zhī wài méiyǒu qítā duōyú de dōngxī. Xiànzài yòng lái xíngróng rén de pínkùn.

Gùshì: Láiyuán yú "jìn shū". Zài gǔ shíhòu, yǒu yīgè dúshūrén, tā de míngzì jiào wáng gōng, tā cónglái dōu bù tāntú xiǎngshòu, guòzhe jíqí púsù de shēnghuó. Rénmen juédé tā jiānglái yīdìng néng chéngwéi yīgè lìhài de rénwù. Yǒu yīcì, tā de fùqīn dàizhe tā qùle wàidì, yǒu yīgè lǎoxiāng guòlái kànwàng tā, tāmen liáo dé shífēn kāixīn. Liáozhe liáozhe zhè wèi lǎoxiāng juédé zuòzhe de zhú xí hěn shūfú, tā xīnlǐ xiǎng wáng gōng cóng shèngchǎn zhú xí de jiāxiāng guòlái, yīdìng dàile hěnduō zhèyàng de zhú xí, yúshì xiǎng wèn tā yào yī zhāngzhúxí. Jiù shuō:"Zhège zhú xí zuòzhe gǎnjué hěn shūfú.", Wáng gōng lìmǎ míngbáile tā de yìsi, xiàozhe shuō:"Nà jiù bǎ zhège sòng gěi nǐ ba." Lǎoxiāng hěn gāoxìng de bǎ zhú xí dài huí jiāle. Qíshí wáng gōng zhǐyǒu zhè yīgè zhú xí, lǎoxiāng bǎ zhú xí dài zǒu hòu, tā jiù yòng cǎo xí shuìjiào. Lǎoxiāng dé zhīliǎo zhè jiàn shìqíng zhīhòu, xīnlǐ gǎnjué hěn guòyìbùqù, jiù qù zhǎo wáng gōng dàoqiàn, wáng gōng xiàozhe shuō:"Nǐ kěnéng bù tài liǎojiě wǒ, wǒ zhè yīshēng méiyǒu tài duō de duōyú de dōngxī."

Chapter 5: Incurable

Idiom: 不可救药。

Pinyin: Bù kě jiù yào.

English: Incurable; hopeless; extremely ill; one is so seriously ill that can't be cured with medicine; dying ill; about to die.

Source: From "The Book of Songs·Daya·Ban".

出处: 《诗经·大雅·板》。

Chūchù: "Shījīng·dàyǎ·bǎn".

不	Bù	No; not
可	Kě	Can; may
救	Jiù	Rescue; save
药	Yào	Medicine; drug; remedy

English

King Li (周厉王/厉王) of the Western Zhou Dynasty （西周） lived a luxurious and prosperous life. He was arrogant who cruelly oppressed and exploited the people. At that time, there was a loyal official named Fan Bo (凡伯), who often risked his life to give good advice to the king. However, the King Li would not listen at all. Those treacherous ministers, who favored by King Li, would often laugh at Fan Bo.

Seeing the country's decline, Fan Bo was very anxious in his heart, so he wrote a poem to warn the treacherous group. The central idea of the poem is as follows:

"I didn't say these words because I am old or stupid,
Well, I'd better prevent a trouble before it came;
If the trouble accumulates,
Like a burning flame, there'd be no way to save it."

Sure enough, after a while, the people finally couldn't bear the oppression by the king. They rushed into the palace and drove King Zhou Li to a far place. King Zhou Li stayed there for fourteen years until he died. The king could have avoided his unfortunate end by being kind. But he didn't listen to Fan Bo's suggestion. Hence, his situation became incurable.

中文

1	严重	Yánzhòng	Serious; grave; grievous; critical
2	已经	Yǐjīng	Already
3	办法	Bànfǎ	Method; means; measure
4	医治	Yīzhì	Cure; treat; heal; give medical treatment
5	地步	Dìbù	Condition; plight; situation; state
6	无法	Wúfǎ	Unable; incapable
7	挽回	Wǎnhuí	Retrieve; redeem
8	从前	Cóngqián	Before; formerly; in the past; once upon a time
9	君王	Jūnwáng	King; lord
10	奢靡	Shēmí	Extravagant; wasteful
11	剥削	Bōxuè	Exploit
12	欺压	Qīyā	Bully and oppress; ride roughshod over
13	人民	Rénmín	The people
14	忠臣	Zhōngchén	Official loyal to his sovereign
15	根本	Gēnběn	Root; radical; basic;

			fundamental
16	进去	Jìnqù	Go in; get in; enter; in
17	器重	Qìzhòng	Think highly of; regard highly; have a high opinion of
18	奸臣	Jiānchén	Treacherous court official; traitor minister
19	嘲笑	Cháoxiào	Ridicule; deride; jeer at; make fun of
20	越来越	Yuè lái yuè	More and more
21	衰败	Shuāibài	Decline; wane; be on the wane; fall into decay
22	着急	Zhāojí	Worry; feel anxious
23	于是	Yúshì	Thereupon; hence; consequently; as a result
24	警告	Jǐnggào	Warn; caution; admonish; warning
25	大概	Dàgài	General idea; broad outline
26	意思是	Yìsi shì	Mean; to the effect that
27	刚刚	Gānggāng	Just; only; exactly
28	到来	Dàolái	Arrival; advent
29	还可以	Hái kěyǐ	Not bad; passable; in addition
30	制止	Zhìzhǐ	Restrain; check; stop; repress
31	放任	Fàngrèn	Not interfere; let go unchecked; let alone
32	燃烧	Ránshāo	Burn; kindle; flame; set on fire
33	火焰	Huǒyàn	Flame; blaze

34	越来越强大	Yuè lái yuè qiángdà	From strength to strength; become stronger and stronger
35	到最后	Dào zuìhòu	In the end; to the end; in the ultimate
36	治理	Zhìlǐ	Administer; govern; run; manage
37	只能	Zhǐ néng	Can only
38	毁灭	Huǐmiè	Destroy; exterminate; ruin
39	果然	Guǒrán	Really; as expected; sure enough
40	不久以后	Bùjiǔ yǐhòu	Soon afterwards; before long; by and by; shortly afterwards; not long after
41	百姓	Bǎixìng	Common people; people
42	不再	Bù zài	No longer; not any more
43	忍受	Rěnshòu	Bear; endure; undergo; suffer
44	造反	Zàofǎn	Rise in rebellion; rebel; revolt
45	冲进	Chōng jìn	Burst in; rush in
46	皇宫	Huánggōng	Imperial palace; palace
47	流放	Liúfàng	Banish; send into exile; exile; float downstream
48	很远	Hěn yuǎn	A long way off; far away; far from; so far
49	地方	Dìfāng	Place; space; room; locality; local
50	直到	Zhídào	Until

51	去世	Qùshì	Die; pass away
52	危机	Wéijī	Crisis; crunch
53	时候	Shíhòu	Time
54	采取措施	Cǎiqǔ cuòshī	Take steps; take measures; take measures to; take a step; adopt measures
55	解决	Jiějué	Solve; resolve; settle; finish off
56	就会	Jiù huì	Will; would have;
57	无法	Wúfǎ	Unable; incapable

译意：得了很严重的病已经到了没有办法医治的地步。比喻事情到了无法挽回的地步。

故事：从前有个君王，他生活奢靡，残酷地剥削和欺压人民。有一个忠臣劝诫他，他根本听不进去。其他被器重的奸臣都嘲笑这个忠臣。忠臣看着国家越来越衰败，非常着急。于是写了一首诗来警告君王。大概意思是：在危机刚刚到来时，还可以制止，如果放任它不管，它就会像燃烧的火焰一样，越来越强大，到最后没有办法治理，只能被毁灭。果然，不久以后，被欺压的百姓不再忍受，开始造反，冲进皇宫里，把君王流放到很远的地方，直到他去世。

启发：在危机刚刚开始的时候就采取措施解决它，拖到最后就会无法挽回。

Pinyin

Yì yì: Déliǎo hěn yánzhòng de bìng yǐjīng dàole méiyǒu bànfǎ yīzhì dì dìbù. Bǐyù shìqíng dào liǎo wúfǎ wǎnhuí dì dìbù.

Gùshì: Cóngqián yǒu gè jūnwáng, tā shēnghuó shēmí, cánkù de bōxuè hé qīyā rénmín. Yǒu yīgè zhōngchén quànjiè tā, tā gēnběn tīng bù jìnqù. Qítā bèi qìzhòng de jiānchén dōu cháoxiào zhège zhōngchén. Zhōngchén kànzhe guójiā yuè lái yuè shuāibài, fēicháng zhāojí. Yúshì xiěle yī shǒu shī lái jǐnggào jūnwáng. Dàgài yìsi shì: Zài wéijī gānggāng dàolái shí, hái kěyǐ zhìzhǐ, rúguǒ fàngrèn tā bùguǎn, tā jiù huì xiàng ránshāo de huǒyàn yīyàng, yuè lái yuè qiángdà, dào zuìhòu méiyǒu bànfǎ zhìlǐ, zhǐ néng bèi huǐmiè. Guǒrán, bùjiǔ yǐhòu, bèi qīyā de bǎixìng bù zài rěnshòu, kāishǐ zàofǎn, chōng jìn huánggōng lǐ, bǎ jūnwáng liúfàng dào hěn yuǎn dì dìfāng, zhídào tā qùshì.

Qǐfā: Zài wéijī gānggāng kāishǐ de shíhòu jiù cǎiqǔ cuòshī jiějué tā, tuō dào zuìhòu jiù huì wúfǎ wǎnhuí.

Chapter 6: Stretched

Idiom: 捉襟见肘。

Pinyin: Zhuō jīn jiàn zhǒu.

English: To be stretched; to have no clue to deal with a situation; to have too many problems and not being able to deal with them; ragged clothes, full of holes and sore; being exhausted. The idiom describes the clothes as tattered-- Pulling the front of the shirt reveals the elbows. It is an analogy of taking care of this and losing that (the other things), and being too poor to deal with it.

Source: (Pre-Qin) Zhuang Zhou " Zhuangzi ·Rangwang".

出处:（先秦）庄周《庄子·让王》。

Chūchù: (Xiānqín) zhuāng zhōu "Zhuāngzi·ràng wáng".

捉	Zhuō	Hold; seize
襟	Jīn	Front of a garment
见	Jiàn	See; meet with

肘	Zhǒu	Elbow

English

Zeng Zi (曾子/曾参) was a native of Lu State (鲁国) during the Spring and Autumn Period. He was a disciple of Confucius and had a lot of knowledge.

His lived a very secluded and miserable life. It is said that when he lived in Wei State (卫国), his life was very difficult. The robe he wore was very shabby. It was made of fluffy linen, and the robe has a very poor quality of fabric. He often had no food in his abdomen, his face was swollen, and his hands and feet were covered with calluses. He often didn't cook for days. He didn't get a new dress for nearly 10 years. The hat he wore hadn't been changed for several years, and even when he wore a hat, the straps of the hat would break when he'd put it on. The clothes he was wore were in tatters, and his elbows were exposed as soon as he'd put on the shirt.

Later generations often say that Confucius had "70 wise men and 3,000 disciples" (贤人七十，弟子三千). Zeng Zi was one of the wise men who is still highly respected by the Chinese people. Although Zeng Zi's life was unbearable, he always maintained an optimistic spirit. According to historical records, he often gave lectures in shabby shoes that did not match his feet.

However, his voice was as loud as a beating of gold and stones, spreading all over the world.

中文

1	衣服	Yīfú	Clothing; clothes; dress
2	就会	Jiù huì	Will; would have
3	露出	Lùchū	Show; reveal
4	胳膊肘	Gēbó zhǒu	Elbow
5	衣着	Yīzhuó	Clothing, headgear and footwear
6	破旧	Pòjiù	Old and shabby; worn-out; dilapidated

7	曾参	Zēngshēn	One of the disciples of Confucius in his later years, an important representative of the Confucian school (505-435 BC); also known as Zeng Zi (曾子)
8	得了	Déliǎo	Stop it; hold it
9	这边	Zhè biān	This side; here
10	那边	Nà biān	There; over there
11	春秋	Chūnqiū	Spring and autumn; year; age; annals
12	时期	Shíqí	Period
13	一个人	Yīgè rén	One
14	孔子	Kǒngzǐ	Confucius
15	优秀	Yōuxiù	Outstanding; excellent; splendid; fine
16	学生	Xuéshēng	Student; pupil; disciple; follower
17	十分	Shífēn	Very; fully; utterly; extremely
18	艰苦	Jiānkǔ	Arduous; difficult; hard; tough
19	生活	Shēnghuó	Life; live; exist; livelihood
20	贫困	Pínkùn	Poor; impoverished; poverty-stricken; in

			straitened circumstances
21	有时候	Yǒu shíhòu	There are times when
22	吃不上	Chībùshàng	Be unable to get something to eat
23	一顿饭	Yī dùn fàn	Meal
24	一年到头	Yīniándàotóu	Throughout the year; in season and out of season; year in, year out; the whole year
25	没有	Méiyǒu	Not have; there is not; be without; not so ...as
26	新衣服	Xīn yīfú	New clothes; New Clothes; a bland new coat
27	整理	Zhěnglǐ	Arrange; put in order; reorganize; sort out
28	一下	Yīxià	One time; once
29	鞋子	Xiézi	Shoes
30	脚后跟	Jiǎohòugēn	Heel
31	穿着	Chuānzhuó	Dress; apparel; what one wears
32	破烂	Pòlàn	Tattered; ragged; worn-out; junk
33	但是	Dànshì	But; however; yet; still
34	丝毫	Sīháo	The slightest amount or degree; a bit; a particle; a shred

35	不在意	Bù zàiyì	Pay no attention to; take no notice of; not to mind
36	自由自在	Zìyóu zìzài	Take one's ease; be one's own man; able to do anything of one's own free will; at liberty
37	即使	Jíshǐ	Even; even if; even though
38	主动	Zhǔdòng	Initiative; driving
39	权贵	Quánguì	Influential officials; bigwigs
40	结交	Jiéjiāo	Make friends with; associate with
41	自己	Zìjǐ	Oneself; of one's own side; closely related
42	自由	Zìyóu	Freedom; liberty; free; unrestrained

译意：扯一扯衣服就会露出胳膊肘，比喻衣着破旧不堪。同时比喻顾得了这边顾不了那边。

故事：在春秋时期，有一个人叫曾参，他是孔子门下的一位优秀的学生。他过得十分艰苦，生活贫困。有时候好几天都吃不上一顿饭，一年到头都没有一件新衣服穿。他穿的衣服整理一下就会露出胳膊肘，鞋子提一下就会露出脚后跟，穿着十分破烂。但是他却丝毫不在意这些，每天哼着歌，过着自由自在的生活。即使生活贫困，他也没有主动与权贵结交，自己过着自由的生活。

Pinyin

Yì yì: Chě yī chě yīfú jiù huì lùchū gēbó zhǒu, bǐyù yīzhuó pòjiù bùkān. Tóngshí bǐyù gù déliǎo zhè biān gù bùliǎo nà biān.

Gùshì: Zài chūnqiū shíqí, yǒuyī gèrén jiào zēngshēn, tā shì kǒngzǐ ménxià de yī wèi yōuxiù de xuéshēng. Tāguò dé shífēn jiānkǔ, shēnghuó pínkùn. Yǒu shíhòu hǎo jǐ tiān dū chībùshàng yī dùn fàn, yīniándàotóu dōu méiyǒu yī jiàn xīn yīfú chuān. Tā chuān de yīfú zhěnglǐ yīxià jiù huì lùchū gēbó zhǒu, xiézi tí yīxià jiù huì lùchū jiǎohòugēn, chuānzhuó shífēn pòlàn. Dànshì tā què sīháo bù zàiyì zhèxiē, měitiān hēngzhe gē,guòzhe zìyóu zìzài de shēnghuó. Jíshǐ shēnghuó pínkùn, tā yě méiyǒu zhǔdòng yǔ quánguì jiéjiāo, zìjǐguòzhe zìyóu de shēnghuó.

Chapter 7: Arrogant

Idiom: 趾高气昂/趾高气扬。

Pinyin: Zhǐ gāo qì'áng/zhǐ gāo qì yáng.

English: Pompous; arrogant; feet are lifted high when walking, and they are full of air.

Source: "Zuǒ chuán·huángōng shísān nián".

出处：《左传·桓公十三年》。

Chūchù: "Zuo Zhuan·Thirteen Years of Huan Gong".

趾	Zhǐ	Toe; foot
高	Gāo	Tall; high
气	Qì	Gas; air; breath
昂	Áng	Hold high; raise
扬	Yáng	Raise; spread

English

In the Spring and Autumn Period, there was a general named Qu Xia (屈瑕) in the Chu State (楚国). He was an ignorant person who paid special attention to appearance（外貌）of others.

Even for the small achievements, he used to feel proud and complacent. Once, he defeated the powerful Jiaoguo（绞国）and returned triumphantly. From then on, he was so proud and content that he never cared about the threats from the other courtiers.

The next year, Qu Xia was ordered to go to repeal the army of Kingdom of Luo. A general named Dou Bobi（斗伯比）went to see him off. When Dou Bobi came back, he quietly said to the cart driver: " General Qu is sure to lose this battle. Because I can see from the way he walks that his heart is not really used for fighting, but to frighten the enemy. How can he win the battle in this way?"

After Dou Bobi finished speaking, he pondered for a while, went into the palace to see the Chu King, and asked the King to send troops to respond immediately. The king of Chu did not believe him, so he went back to his harem and told his concubine Dengman (邓曼) about the matter. Dengman thought Dou Bobi was right and advised the King to send troops to rescue Qu Xia and deal with the war.

The King heard this and immediately dispatched a large army, hoping to resolve the situation. However, the war had already taken place. Qu Xia could not defend himself because he underestimated the enemy, and was attacked by Luo and Lu States (罗国和卢国). He suffered a crushing defeat, and had to commit suicide.

Since then, this story has been passed down from generations to generations, and the posture of walking proudly has also been extended to the phrase "high and mighty" (趾高气扬), which is a metaphor for a person's arrogance and contentment, without caring about anyone.

中文

1	一个人	Yīgè rén	One
2	走路	Zǒulù	Walk; go on foot
3	十分	Shífēn	Very; fully; utterly; extremely
4	神气	Shénqì	Expression; air; manner
5	骄傲自大	Jiāo'ào zì dà	Arrogant; be bloated with pride; feel high and mighty; get a swelled head
6	过分	Guòfèn	Excessive; undue; bellyful; go too far
7	得意	Déyì	Proud of oneself; pleased with oneself
8	在古代	Zài gǔdài	In ancient times; in the old days; in the ancient time
9	将军	Jiāngjūn	General; admiral
10	注重	Zhùzhòng	Lay stress on; lay emphasis on; pay attention to; emphasize
11	表面	Biǎomiàn	Surface; superficies; boundary; face
12	功夫	Gōngfū	Workmanship; skill; art; ability
13	有一次	Yǒu yīcì	Once; on one occasion
14	领兵	Lǐng bīng	Lead troops

15	作战	Zuòzhàn	Fight; conduct operations; do battle; show
16	打败	Dǎbài	Defeat; beat; worst
17	敌国	Díguó	Enemy state; hostile country; hostile power
18	于是	Yúshì	Thereupon; hence; consequently; as a result
19	十分	Shífēn	Very; fully; utterly; extremely
20	回到	Huí dào	Return to; go back to
21	自己的	Zìjǐ de	Self
22	国家	Guójiā	Country; state; nation
23	不放在眼里	Bù fàng zài yǎn lǐ	Look down upon; treat somebody anyway one pleases
24	觉得	Juédé	Feel; be aware; sense
25	自己	Zìjǐ	Oneself; of one's own side; closely related
26	非常	Fēicháng	Extraordinary; unusual; special; very
27	厉害	Lìhài	Severe; sharp; cruel; fierce
28	后来	Hòulái	Afterwards; later; then
29	军队	Jūnduì	Armed forces; army; troops; host
30	过来	Guòlái	Come over; come up; can manage

31	皇帝	Huángdì	Emperor
32	出战	Chūzhàn	Go out to fight; go to war; enter the arena
33	高兴地	Gāoxìng de	With a heart and a half; with delight; with pleasure
34	出发	Chū fā	Set out; start off; leave;
35	送行	Sòng xíng	See somebody off; wish somebody bon voyage; say goodbye to somebody
36	看到	Kàn dào	See; catch sight of
37	样子	Yàngzi	Appearance; shape
38	回去	Huíqù	Return; go back; be back; back
39	步子	Bùzi	Step; pace; footstep
40	大大	Dàdà	Greatly; enormously
41	打仗	Dǎzhàng	Fight; go to war; make war
42	而是	Ér shì	Not A, but B
43	吓唬	Xiàhǔ	Frighten; scare; intimidate; browbeat
44	对面	Duìmiàn	Opposite; across the way
45	敌人	Dírén	Enemy; foe
46	而已	Éryǐ	That is all; nothing more
47	战争	Zhànzhēng	War; warfare
48	很可能	Hěn kěnéng	Very likely
49	失败	Shībài	Be defeated; lose; fail; come

			to nothing
50	请求	Qǐngqiú	Ask; request; demand; beg
51	出兵	Chūbīng	Dispatch troops; march army for battle; send an army into battle
52	增援	Zēngyuán	Reinforce
53	赞同	Zàntóng	Approve of; agree with; endorse; go along with
54	支援	Zhīyuán	Support; assist; help; aid
55	到达	Dàodá	Arrive; get to; reach
56	战场	Zhànchǎng	Battlefield; battleground; battlefront
57	已经	Yǐjīng	Already
58	结束	Jiéshù	Finish; closure; foreclosure; end
59	过于	Guòyú	Too; unduly; excessively
60	轻敌	Qīngdí	Take the enemy lightly; underestimate the enemy
61	羞愧	Xiūkuì	Ashamed; abashed
62	自杀	Zìshā	Commit suicide; take one's own life
63	不论	Bùlùn	No matter what; regardless of
64	取得	Qǔdé	Acquire; gain; obtain
65	怎样	Zěnyàng	How
66	成就	Chéngjiù	Achievement;

			accomplishment; attainment; success
67	不要	Bùyào	Don't
68	骄傲自满	Jiāo'ào zìmǎn	Be big with pride; be complacent; be conceited and complacent; conceited and self-complacent
69	别人	Biérén	Other people; others; people
70	眼里	Yǎn lǐ	Within one's vision; in one's eyes
71	这样	Zhèyàng	So; such; like this; this way
72	造成	Zàochéng	Give rise to; bring about; create; cause
73	后果	Hòuguǒ	Consequence; aftermath
74	可能	Kěnéng	Possible; probable; can; may
75	导致	Dǎozhì	Cause; lead to; bring about; result in

译意：一个人走路时把脚抬得很高，十分神气。比喻骄傲自大，过分得意的样子。

故事：在古代有一位将军，是一个只注重表面功夫的人。有一次他领兵作战，打败了敌国的军队，于是他十分得意，回到自己的国家后十分神气，谁都不放在眼里，觉得自己非常厉害。后来又有敌国军队攻过来，皇帝派他出战。他高兴地出发了，有一位送行的人看到他走路的样子十分神气，回去就向皇帝说："将军出发时头仰得高高的，步子迈的大大的，十分神气，看样子不是去打仗而是只想吓唬吓唬对面的敌人而已，这场战争很可能会失败，请求皇帝出兵增援。"皇帝听了，也十分赞同，于是派兵去支援，结果到达战场时，战争已经结束，将军太过于轻敌，而被敌人打败了，自己觉得羞愧于是就自杀了。

启发：不论取得怎样的成就，都不要太骄傲自满，不把别人放在眼里，这样会造成不好的后果，可能导致你最终失败。

Pinyin

Yì yì: Yīgè rén zǒulù shí bǎ jiǎo tái dé hěn gāo, shífēn shénqì. Bǐyù jiāo'ào zì dà, guòfèn déyì de yàngzi.

Gùshì: Zài gǔdài yǒuyī wèi jiāngjūn, shì yīgè zhǐ zhùzhòng biǎomiàn gōngfū de rén. Yǒuyīcì tā lǐng bīng zuòzhàn, dǎbàile díguó de jūnduì, yúshì tā shífēn déyì, huí dào zìjǐ de guójiā hòu shífēn shénqì, shéi dōu bù fàng zài yǎn lǐ, juédé zìjǐ fēicháng lìhài. Hòulái yòu yǒu díguó jūnduì gōng guòlái, huángdì pài tā chūzhàn. Tā gāoxìng dì chūfāle, yǒu yī wèi sòngxíng de rén kàn dào tā zǒulù de yàngzi shífēn shénqì, huíqù jiù xiàng huángdì shuō:"Jiāngjūn chūfā shí tóu yǎng dé gāo gāo de, bùzi mài de dàdà de, shífēn shénqì, kàn yàngzi bùshì qù dǎzhàng ér shì zhǐ xiǎng xiàhǔ xiàhǔ duìmiàn de dírén éryǐ, zhè chǎng zhànzhēng hěn kěnéng huì shībài, qǐngqiú huángdì chūbīng zēngyuán." Huángdì tīngle, yě shífēn zàntóng, yúshì pàibīng qù zhīyuán, jiéguǒ dàodá zhànchǎng shí, zhànzhēng yǐjīng jiéshù, jiāngjūn tài guòyú qīngdí, ér bèi dírén dǎbàile, zìjǐ juédé xiūkuì yúshì jiù zìshāle.

Qǐfā: Bùlùn qǔdé zěnyàng de chéngjiù, dōu bùyào tài jiāo'ào zìmǎn, bù bǎ biérén fàng zài yǎn lǐ, zhèyàng huì zàochéng bù hǎo de hòuguǒ, kěnéng dǎozhì nǐ zuìzhōng shībài.

Chapter 8: Be Prepared

Idiom: 有备无患。

Pinyin: Yǒu bèi wú huàn.

English: Be prepared and you won't be sorry; have a second string to one's bow; if one is prepared, he will be safe.

Source: "Shangshu·Shuo Ming".

出处:《尚书·说命》

Chūchù: "Shàngshū·shuō mìng".

有	Yǒu	Have; possess
备	Bèi	Be equipped with; prepare
无	Wú	Not have; be without
患	Huàn	Trouble; peril; disaster

English

In the Spring and Autumn Period, after Duke Dao of Jin (晋悼公) became the monarch, he wanted to regain the lost reputation of the Jin State (晋国) and become a ruler like his predecessor, Duke Wen of Jin (晋文公). At this time, Zheng State (郑国) was a small country. One moment, Zheng allied with Jin, and the next moment, Zheng turned to Chu for friendship.

Duke Dao of Jin was very angry. In 562 BC, he gathered troops from 11 countries including Song (宋), Lu (鲁), Wei (卫), and Liu (刘) and sent troops to attack the Zheng State. The defeated Zeng quickly surrendered and sent a large number of gifts to Jin, including 100 military vehicles, several musicians, a group of precious musical instruments, and 16 women who were good at singing and dancing.

Duke Dao of Jin was very happy and gave half of these gifts to Wei Jiang (魏绛, a general who was good at leading troops in the battles), saying: "Wei Jiang, it was you who persuaded me to make peace with Rong and Di (戎狄) that brought stability to the central Plains. Over the past eight years, we have convened nine meetings of princes. Now our relationship with other countries is as harmonious as a beautiful piece of music. Zheng State has sent so many gifts, let me share it with you!"

Wei Jiang said, "It is a blessing for our country to be able to get along well with Di and Rong. Your Majesty is the leader of the central plains. It is because of your ability-- I have made little contribution. This is based on your talents. My effort is insignificant. However, I hope you can think more about the future of your country while enjoying yourself. In the Book of History 《尚书》, it says: 'When you are settling down, you should think of the danger that may happen in the future. If you think of it, you will be prepared. If you are prepared, there will be no disaster.' I would like to use these words to remind your Majesty!"

中文

| 1 | 平时 | Píngshí | In normal times; at ordinary times; in peacetime |
| 2 | 有所 | Yǒu suǒ | To some extent; somewhat |

3	遇到	Yù dào	Run into; encounter; come across
4	突发事件	Tú fā shìjiàn	Emergency; incident; emergency events
5	才能	Cáinéng	Talent; ability; gift; aptitude
6	在古代	Zài gǔdài	In ancient times; in the old days; in the ancient time
7	强大	Qiángdà	Big and powerful; powerful; formidable
8	君王	Jūnwáng	King; lord
9	联合	Liánhé	Unite; ally; alliance; union
10	其他	Qítā	Other; else
11	攻打	Gōngdǎ	Attack; assault; assail
12	敌国	Díguó	Enemy state; hostile country; hostile power
13	军力	Jūnlì	Military strength
14	抵抗	Dǐkàng	Resist; stand up to; oppose; resistance
15	大批	Dàpī	Large quantities of; a smart of
16	贵重	Guìzhòng	Valuable; precious
17	礼物	Lǐwù	Gift; present
18	乐器	Yuèqì	Musical instrument; instrument; axe
19	美貌	Měimào	Beautiful
20	舞女	Wǔnǚ	Taxi dancer; dancing girl; dance-hostess

21	很高兴	Hěn gāoxìng	Delighted; very happy; With pleasure
22	收下	Shōu xià	Accept; receive
23	同意	Tóngyì	Agree; consent; approve; agreement
24	战争	Zhànzhēng	War; warfare
25	分给	Fēn gěi	Give (a share to sb.); impart
26	大臣	Dàchén	Minister; secretary
27	站出来	Zhàn chūlái	Step forward; step forward bravely; come out boldly
28	大王	Dàwáng	King; monarch; magnate
29	才能	Cáinéng	Talent; ability; gift; aptitude
30	出众	Chūzhòng	Be out of the ordinary; be outstanding; exceptional
31	臣服	Chénfú	Submit oneself to the rule of; acknowledge allegiance to
32	但是	Dànshì	But; however; yet; still
33	提醒	Tíxǐng	Remind; warn; call attention to; prompting
34	一下	Yīxià	One time; once
35	不要	Bùyào	Don't
36	沉迷于	Chénmí yú	Indulge; be addicted to; be rapt in
37	享乐	Xiǎnglè	Lead a life of pleasure; indulge in creature comforts
38	考虑	Kǎolǜ	Think over; take into account;

			consider; regard
39	未来	Wèilái	Coming; approaching; next; future
40	突发	Tú fā	Burst out; occur suddenly
41	紧急情况	Jǐnjí qíngkuàng	Emergency; critical situation; emergency case
42	准备	Zhǔnbèi	Prepare; get ready; intend; plan
43	应对	Yìngduì	Reply; answer
44	这样	Zhèyàng	So; such; like this; this way
45	我们的	Wǒmen de	Ours
46	更加	Gèngjiā	To a higher degree; still further; still more
47	繁荣昌盛	Fánróng chāngshèng	Thriving and prosperous; flourishing and invigorating

译意：平时有所准备，遇到突发事件才能从容应对。

故事：在古代有一个强大的国家，他的君王联合其他小国家攻打敌国，敌国军力不足以抵抗，于是就派人求和，送了他们大批的贵重礼物，有乐器和美貌的舞女。君王很高兴，将这些礼物收下了，同意暂时停止战争。他将这些礼物分给他的大臣，有一位大臣站出来说："大王的才能出众，才让敌国臣服于我们，但是我想提醒一下大王，不要沉迷于享乐，要多考虑一下国家的未来，这样才能在国家遇到突发的紧急情况时，有所准备，可以应对，这样我们的国家才会更加繁荣昌盛"。

Pinyin

Yì yì: Píngshí yǒu suǒ zhǔnbèi, yù dào tú fā shìjiàn cáinéng cóngróng yìngduì.

Gùshì: Zài gǔdài yǒuyīgè qiángdà de guójiā, tā de jūnwáng liánhé qítā xiǎo guójiā gōngdǎ díguó, díguó jūnlì bùzú yǐ dǐkàng, yúshì jiù pài rén qiú hé, sòngle tāmen dàpī de guìzhòng lǐwù, yǒu yuèqì hé měimào de wǔnǚ. Jūnwáng hěn gāoxìng, jiāng zhèxiē lǐwù shōu xiàle, tóngyì zhànshí tíngzhǐ zhànzhēng. Tā jiāng zhèxiē lǐwù fēn gěi tā de dàchén, yǒu yī wèi dàchén zhàn chūlái shuō:"Dàwáng de cáinéng chūzhòng, cái ràng díguó chénfú yú wǒmen, dànshì wǒ xiǎng tíxǐng yīxià dàwáng, bùyào chénmí yú xiǎnglè, yào duō kǎolǜ yīxià guójiā de wèilái, zhèyàng cáinéng zài guójiā yù dào tú fā de jǐnjí qíngkuàng shí, yǒu suǒ zhǔnbèi, kěyǐ yìngduì, zhèyàng wǒmen de guójiā cái huì gèngjiā fánróng chāngshèng".

Chapter 9: Stopgap

Idiom: 滥竽充数。
Pinyin: Làn yú chōng shù.

English: People who have no real talents can mix among talented and get rewarded. Someone who doesn't know how to play the ribbon, can get rewards by pretending to be mixed in a 300-member band, but when he has to play alone to demonstrate his real skills, he has to escape; act as a stopgap; be dragged in to swell the total; fill a post without real qualifications.

Source: "Han Feizi: Internal Reserve".
出处:《韩非子·内储说上》。
Chūchù: "Hánfēizi·nèi chǔ shuō shàng".

滥	Làn	Overflow; flood; inundate; excessively; indiscriminately; immoderately; without restraint; shoddy; hackneyed; stale; trite
竽	Yú	An ancient wind instrument; 36-reed wind instrument

| 充 | Chōng | Sufficient; full; ample; fill; charge; stuff; serve as |
| 数 | Shù | Number; figure; fate; destiny; several; a few |

English

During the Warring States Period, King Qi Xuan (齐宣王, 350 BC-301 BC; real name: Tian Piqiang, 田辟彊, Tián pì jiàng) liked to listen to people playing the Yu (竽, an ancient wind instrument) very much. The King liked many musicians to ensemble for him, so King Qi Xuan sent his ministers everywhere to search for the musicians who were good at playing Yu. Finally, a band of 300 musicians was formed. These musicians were given a particularly generous treatment, such as entering the palace.

At that time, there was a lazy man surnamed Nan Guo (南郭, a two character surname). He had no interest in working hard. When Mr. Nan Guo heard that King Qi Xuan had such a hobby, he wanted to get involved in the band.

So, he met King Qi Xuan and boasted to the King that he was a great musician. He won the favor of King. As a result, King Xuan also included him in the music band.

As a matter of fact, Mr. Nan Guo didn't know how to play Yu at all. Whenever the band played for King Qi Xuan, he would mix in the team, imitating the other musicians, shaking his head, shaking his hands, and pretending to perform there well. As Mr. Nan Guo learned to pretend so well, and since always hundreds of people performed together, the King couldn't hear anything unusual. In this way, several years passed away. Not only Mr. Nan Guo managed to hide his flaws, but he also, like other musicians, received generous rewards from the King. This way, Mr. Nan Guo lived a very comfortable life for a long time.

Later, when King Qi Xuan died, his son (real name Tian Sui, 田遂, Tián suì) succeeded to the throne as King Min of Qi (齐湣王, Qí mǐn wáng).

King Min of Qi also liked to listen to the music. However, there was only one difference with respect to his late father's interest in music: King Min didn't like ensemble, rather he liked to listen to the musicians one by one.

When Mr. Nan Guo learned about the new king, he got so scared that he started sweating. He trembled all day long as if he was walking on the thin ice. Mr. Nan Guo thought: "it's better to resign and lose his job, if I am accused of deceiving the King King Qi Xuan, I may even get executed, so it is totally fine to disappear as soon as possible." So, before the new King would ask him to play, Mr. Nan Guo quickly slipped away.

Finally, Mr. Nan Guo realized that although the method of falsification can be exchanged for temporary success, it cannot be exchanged for the success of a lifetime. People can only achieve real success if they work hard and have true talents.

中文

1	不会	Bù huì	Will not; not likely; incapable

2	乐师	Yuèshī	Musician
3	团队	Tuánduì	Team; group; corps
4	假装	Jiǎzhuāng	Pretend; feign; simulate; make believe
5	自己	Zìjǐ	Oneself; of one's own side; closely related
6	比喻	Bǐyù	Metaphor or simile; analogy; figure of speech; allegory
7	不符合	Bù fúhé	Inconformity
8	真实	Zhēnshí	True; real; authentic
9	情况	Qíngkuàng	Circumstances; situation; condition; state of affairs
10	指的是	Zhǐ de shì	Refer to…; mean; social order; Nobody
11	没有	Méiyǒu	Not have; there is not; be without; not so …as
12	才华	Cáihuá	Literary or artistic talent; rich talent; talent; gifts
13	战国	Zhànguó	Warring States
14	时期	Shíqí	Period
15	君王	Jūnwáng	King; lord
16	很喜欢	Hěn xǐhuān	Love
17	演奏	Yǎnzòu	Give an instrumental performance; play a musical instrument

18	乐曲	Yuèqǔ	Musical composition; composition; music
19	到处	Dàochù	At all places; everywhere; in every place; in all places
20	搜集	Sōují	Collect; gather
21	乐队	Yuèduì	Orchestra; band
22	享受	Xiǎngshòu	Enjoyment; comfort; fruition; treat
23	非常好	Fēicháng hǎo	Very good; excellent; very well
24	待遇	Dàiyù	Treatment
25	无所事事	Wúsuǒshìshì	Have nothing to do; be at an idle end; be at loose ends; be occupied with nothing
26	不务正业	Bùwù zhèngyè	Be derelict in duty and run an irrelevant business; not do honest work; not live by honest labour; ignore one's proper occupation
27	试试	Shì shì	Have a try
28	想要	Xiǎng yào	Want; intend; wish
29	进去	Jìnqù	Go in; get in; enter; in
30	于是	Yúshì	Thereupon; hence;

			consequently; as a result
31	面前	Miànqián	In face of; in front of; before
32	吹嘘	Chuīxū	Lavish praise on oneself or others; boast; boost up; glibly profess
33	非常	Fēicháng	Extraordinary; unusual; special; very
34	相信	Xiāngxìn	Believe in; be convinced of; have faith in; take stock in
35	队伍	Duìwǔ	Troops; army
36	可是	Kěshì	But; yet; however
37	根本	Gēnběn	Root; radical; basic; fundamental
38	几百	Jǐ bǎi	Several hundred; hundreds of; Several hundred; a few hundred
39	跟着	Gēnzhe	Follow; in the wake of
40	一起	Yīqǐ	In the same place; together; in company; altogether
41	出来	Chūlái	Come out; emerge
42	就这样	Jiù zhèyàng	That's it; That's all; in this way
43	皇帝	Huángdì	Emperor

44	去世	Qùshì	Die; pass away
45	皇位	Huángwèi	Throne
46	不喜欢	Bù xǐhuān	Dislike
47	独奏	Dúzòu	Solo; pay a solo
48	听说	Tīng shuō	Be told; hear of
49	有一天	Yǒu yītiān	One day; some day
50	不敢	Bù gǎn	Dare not; not dare
51	而是	Ér shì	Not A, but B
52	赶紧	Gǎnjǐn	Lose no time; hasten; run
53	连夜	Liányè	The same night; that very night
54	逃跑	Táopǎo	Run away; flee; escape; take flight

译意：不会吹竽的人混在乐师的团队中假装自己会吹。比喻不符合真实的情况，指的是没有才华的人在有才能的人中混数。

故事：战国时期，有一个君王很喜欢听用竽演奏的乐曲，所以他派人到处搜集会吹竽的人，组成一支三百人的大乐队，来演奏给他听。这些乐师会享受非常好的待遇，有一个每天无所事事，不务正业的人听了，也想去试试，就报了名，想要混进去。于是他在君王面前吹嘘自己非常会吹竽，君王相信了他，于是就把他也编入乐师的队伍中。可是他根本不会吹竽，但是他混在几百人的团队里，跟着其他乐师一起假装演奏也不会被人看出来。所以他就这样在乐师队伍里混了几年。后来这个皇帝去世了，他的儿子继承了他的皇位，他的儿子也喜欢听竽，但是不喜欢太多的人一起演奏，喜欢听独奏，这个人听说了十分害怕自己有一天会暴露，皇帝知道自己不会演奏，就会杀了自己。于是他再也不敢混在乐师队伍中，而是赶紧连夜逃跑了。

Pinyin

Yì yì: Bù huì chuī yú de rén hùnzài yuèshī de tuánduì zhōng jiǎzhuāng zìjǐ huì chuī. Bǐyù bù fúhé zhēnshí de qíngkuàng, zhǐ de shì méiyǒu cáihuá de rén zài yǒu cáinéng de rén zhōng hùn shù.

Gùshì: Zhànguó shíqí, yǒu yīgè jūnwáng hěn xǐhuān tīng yòng yú yǎnzòu de yuèqǔ, suǒyǐ tā pài rén dàochù sōují huì chuī yú de rén, zǔchéng yī zhī sānbǎi rén de dà yuèduì, lái yǎnzòu gěi tā tīng. Zhèxiē yuèshī huì xiǎngshòu fēicháng hǎo de dàiyù, yǒu yīgè měitiān wúsuǒshìshì, bùwùzhèngyè de rén tīngle, yě xiǎng qù shì shì, jiù bàole míng, xiǎng yào hùn jìnqù. Yúshì tā zài jūnwáng miànqián chuīxū zìjǐ fēicháng huì chuī yú, jūnwáng xiāngxìnle tā, yúshì jiù bǎ tā yě biān rù yuèshī de duìwǔ zhōng. Kěshì tā gēnběn bù huì chuī yú, dànshì tā hùnzài jǐ bǎi rén de tuánduì lǐ, gēnzhe qítā yuèshī yīqǐ jiǎzhuāng yǎnzòu yě bù huì bèi rén kàn chūlái. Suǒyǐ tā jiù zhèyàng zài yuèshī duìwǔ lǐ hùnle jǐ nián. Hòulái zhège huángdì qùshìle, tā de érzi jìchéngle tā de huángwèi, tā de érzi yě xǐhuān tīng yú, dànshì bù xǐhuān tài duō de rén yīqǐ yǎnzòu, xǐhuān tīng dúzòu, zhège rén tīng shuōle shífēn hàipà zìjǐ yǒu yītiān huì bàolù, huángdì zhīdào zìjǐ bù huì yǎnzòu, jiù huì shāle zìjǐ. Yúshì tā zài yě bù gǎn hùnzài yuèshī duìwǔ zhōng, ér shì gǎnjǐn liányè táopǎole.

https://ChineseBull.com/

Kexin Su (Nuo Nuo)

苏可馨 (诺诺)

www.ingramcontent.com/pod-product-compliance
Lightning Source LLC
Chambersburg PA
CBHW070623310726
48982CB00001B/162